DISNEP
KINGDOM HEARTS

THE
ULTIMATE
HANDBOOK

BY CONOR LLOYD

SCHOLASTIC INC.

All rights reserved. Published by Scholastic Inc., *Publishers since 1920.* SCHOLASTIC and associated logos are trademarks and/or registered trademarks of Scholastic Inc.

The publisher does not have any control over and does not assume any responsibility for author or third-party websites or their content.

This book is a work of fiction. Names, characters, places, and incidents are either the product of the author's imagination or are used fictitiously, and any resemblance to actual persons, living or dead, business establishments, events, or locales is entirely coincidental.

ISBN: 978-1-338-59618-2

10 9 8 7 6 5 4 3 2 1   20 21 22 23 24
Printed in the U.S.A.   40

First printing 2020

Book design by Jessica Meltzer

TABLE OF CONTENTS

GLOSSARY

KINGDOM HEARTS: The heart of all worlds in the universe, and the source of ultimate power and wisdom. Long ago the universe was whole and full of light. It is said that during this time many people desired the power of Kingdom Hearts, creating the first Keyblades in order to obtain the χ-blade—a powerful weapon that can control Kingdom Hearts. Disputes over the χ-blade caused a massive war that consumed everything in darkness. The χ-blade was shattered into twenty pieces, seven of pure light and thirteen of pure darkness. Kingdom Hearts disappeared into the darkness, and all the worlds in the universe were separated from one another.

AGE OF FAIRY TALES: The time before Kingdom Hearts disappeared into darkness.

χ-BLADE: A legendary weapon that is both the protector and equal of Kingdom Hearts. Many people have searched for it, as the wielder of the χ-Blade can control Kingdom Hearts and thus, all the worlds in the universe.

KEYBLADE: Mysterious sword-like weapons that can only be wielded by people who are strong of heart, called Keyblade Wielders. Keyblades can seal or open the barriers between worlds.

HEARTLESS: Creatures of darkness that desire hearts above all else. They are drawn to people with strong hearts and can even be commanded by those who have learned to control the powers of darkness.

NOBODIES: The body of a strong-willed individual who has lost their heart. When an individual loses his/her heart, a Nobody is created as a separate entity.

ORGANIZATION XIII: A group of thirteen powerful Nobodies who seek to reclaim their hearts and become whole again.

GUARDIANS OF LIGHT: A group of Keyblade wielders who seek to defeat Organization XIII.

THIRTEEN SEEKERS OF DARKNESS: Also called the "Real Organization XIII," this is a group consisting of thirteen different versions of Master Xehanort. They are led by Master Xehanort, who seeks to conquer Kingdom Hearts and re-create the worlds.

REALM OF LIGHT: The side of the universe with an affinity for light.

REALM OF DARKNESS: A realm that lies opposite the Realm of Light. It is inhabited by the Heartless and other dark beings.

THE LAND OF DEPARTURE: One of a few special worlds located between the Realm of Light and the Realm of Darkness. This world is a neutral place where light and darkness exist in balance.

CASTLE OBLIVION: A world located in-between the light realm and the dark realm, and where Organization XIII has traditionally been based.

TRAVERSE TOWN: A refuge in the Realm of Light, survivors of the worlds lost to the Heartless find their way here after their worlds have been destroyed.

GUMMI SHIP: The main method of transportation between worlds. These ships are made of a special material that allows inhabitants to travel between worlds.

INTRODUCTION TO THE HEROES

When the light needs protecting, you know who to turn to! When it comes to saving worlds, it's not just **Keyblade** wielders that know that when the going gets tough the tough get going. Sometimes heroes are big and strong—like Hercules! Some can get the job done by using their brain and thinking their way out of trouble. And some don't even start out as heroes (looking at you, Axel).

But whatever kind of hero you are, as long as you trust in your friends, you can always count on the light getting you through.

"MY FRIENDS ARE MY POWER!"

SORA

Sora is a Keyblade wielder with a big heart. His journey began when his world was swallowed by darkness, separating him from his friends Kairi and Riku. As time went on, Sora ended up visiting many different worlds, making new friends along the way including Donald and Goofy. Sora, Donald, and Goofy faced off against the **Heartless**, **Nobodies**, and other villains as they fought to save worlds from falling into darkness and thwart the plans of **Organization XIII**.

Thanks to the Keyblade, Sora is incredibly capable in combat. He can fight up close or fire off powerful blasts of magic from afar. What's more, Sora is able to summon powerful allies to help him in battle and unleash devastating tandem attacks. Sora is a force to be reckoned with on the battlefield, able to take on over a thousand enemies at once and come out on top!

Sora also has the ability to connect peoples' hearts and minds no matter how far away they are from each other—even if they are in totally different worlds. Thanks to this, Sora is able to bring together warriors of light to face off against the forces of darkness. With his friends at his side, there's nothing Sora can't do.

Sora's Keyblade is from the **Realm of Light** and in its normal form is called the Kingdom Key. However, by equipping it with different keychains, Sora can change its appearance and make it more powerful!

"I KNOW THE WAY. CONSUME THE DARKNESS, RETURN IT TO LIGHT."

RIKU

A Keyblade Master and childhood friend of Sora and Kairi, Riku walks the line between light and darkness. Though he once struggled with the darkness within himself, Riku has learned to harness the power within and now fights to protect his friends and the Realm of Light.

Since Riku mastered the darkness within his heart, he is able to use it in battle—often with explosive results. Riku's dark fire magic is especially powerful, tracking down and homing in on enemies from afar.

Due to his struggles with darkness, Riku often feels guilty, believing that he has betrayed his friends. However, thanks to the support of Sora, Kairi, and King Mickey, Riku realizes that he has nothing to be ashamed of and that his friends will always

be there for him. Riku now uses his powers and mastery of the Keyblade to protect his friends and help maintain the balance between light and dark.

Riku has wielded many different Keyblades, including the Keyblade of People's Hearts, Way to Dawn, and Braveheart.

"THIS TIME . . . I'LL FIGHT. YOU KNOW SORA'S COMPLETELY HOPELESS WITHOUT US! C'MON, RIKU!"

KAIRI

Kairi is a kindhearted but determined person who has frequently found herself at the center of numerous clashes between light and darkness. Due to her pure heart, Kairi's connection to the light is incredibly strong, allowing her to save her friends from the forces of darkness on more than one occasion.

In just a short time wielding a Keyblade, Kairi has proven herself quite adept with the weapon thanks to her training under the legendary wizard Merlin. She has a natural talent for magic and she can use her Keyblade Destiny's Embrace to focus and fire off blasts of energy.

Though she met Sora and Riku on Destiny Island when they were all young, Kairi is originally from a world called Radiant Garden. It was there that she first encountered the Keyblade when she

crossed paths with Master Aqua. During this meeting, Kairi gained the potential to wield the weapon after touching Master Aqua's Keyblade and put a protective charm on Kairi's necklace, further entwining their fates and ensuring that they would one day meet again.

Kairi has a fondness for writing letters and over the course of her adventures has written to Sora a number of times—though she doesn't always mail them!

"LET'S GO GET 'EM, GOOFY!"

DONALD DUCK

Disney Castle's Royal Magician, Donald Duck is a force to be reckoned with. After setting out to search for a Keyblade wielder under orders from King Mickey, he and Goofy run into Sora and quickly become friends.

Thanks to his prodigious magic, Donald is incredibly capable on the battlefield, wielding powerful spells to shock, burn, and blast away foes. He's even able to heal his allies with powerful cure spells, making sure they're healthy, strong, and ready to fight. He has to be careful about managing his power though—slinging too many spells will leave him drained and he'll have to wait before he can use magic again.

Sometimes, Donald's temper can land him in hot water. He and Sora squabble often and on more than one occasion their

fights have gotten out of hand. He has a tendency to charge headfirst into fights without thinking. Despite all that, Donald is fiercely protective of his friends and won't hesitate to help them whenever they're in trouble.

Thanks to Donald's Magic he, Sora, and Goofy are able to blend in no matter what world they end up on. They've transformed into animals, toys, and even monsters!

"A-HYUCK. WE'LL HELP YOU OUT ANY WAY WE CAN."

GOOFY

The happy-go-lucky Captain of the Disney Castle Royal Guard, Goofy has been a faithful member of King Mickey's court for many years. He and Donald Duck set out under Mickey's orders to find the wielder of the Keyblade, and in no time at all they found—and befriended—Sora. They've been almost inseparable ever since, with Goofy acting as the levelheaded balance to Donald and Sora's more hotheaded and airheaded tendencies.

Goofy is a wrecking ball in battle, bowling over enemies with his trusty shield even as he protects his allies from harm. Goofy's resilience and stamina means he can take a hit and get right back up. He can even throw his shield to take out enemies at long range!

While Goofy is clumsy and can be a bit, well, goofy, he is often an important voice of reason. Surprisingly insightful, Goofy is frequently able to find simple solutions to problems that

others—especially Sora and Donald—tend to overlook. Colored with a natural optimism, Goofy is without a doubt the cheerful heart of the team.

Goofy is always trying to cheer people up, either with a corny joke or a silly face!

> **"DON'T WORRY.
> THERE WILL ALWAYS BE
> A DOOR TO THE LIGHT."**

KING MICKEY

A powerful Keyblade Master and the King of Disney Castle, Mickey has been fighting against the darkness for a long time. As Master Yen Sid's apprentice, Mickey learned how to wield both magic and the Keyblade, traveling to many different worlds in order to hone his skills. He has helped Sora on almost all of his adventures, saving him from tight spots time and time again.

Mickey's strength in battle is almost unmatched, as his mastery over both spells and Keyblade techniques is exceptional. His speed allows him to dart around the battlefield and take out foes with lightning speed, while simultaneously dispatching far-off opponents with powerful blasts of energy. Mickey is even able to use the dangerous spell Stopza, allowing him to stop and start time at will. Mickey truly has earned the title of Keyblade Master!

Thanks to the time they shared in the **Realm of Darkness**, Mickey and Riku have a special connection. Together they were able to fight their way back to the Realm of Light. The two make for a powerful pair and their teamwork and trust in each other meant they were able to travel through the Realm of Darkness together to search for Aqua, fighting off powerful Heartless as they went.

Even though he is a warrior of light, Mickey actually wields a Keyblade from the Realm of Darkness, the Kingdom Key D.

"ENOUGH. CHECKMATE."

MASTER ERAQUS

Eraqus is a Keyblade Master who trained in the world Scala ad Caelum in the way of the Keyblade alongside Xehanort. There they forged a strong friendship, though they did not see eye to eye when it came to matters of light and darkness. Eraqus traveled to the **Land of Departure**, where he served as a teacher and guide for the Keyblade Wielders Terra, Ventus, and Aqua. Eventually, Eraqus came to fear the darkness to such an extent that he became blinded by his own light. He was defeated by Terra and then attacked by Xehanort, though he was able to hide his heart within Terra before it could be consumed by darkness. Because of this, he is able to aid Sora and his friends in their final battle against Xehanort.

While he became quite stoic later in life, when he was younger Eraqus was something of a troublemaker.

"SORA . . . YOU'RE LUCKY. LOOKS LIKE MY SUMMER VACATION IS...OVER."

ROXAS

Roxas is Sora's Nobody and a former member of Organization XIII. As Sora's Nobody, Roxas is able to wield the Keyblade and has proven himself an incredibly powerful combatant. While he and Sora are similar, Roxas tends to be more serious, and sometimes has trouble controlling his anger. Though Roxas did reunite with Sora for a time, Sora was able to give him a body of his own.

Roxas has the ability to wield more than one Keyblade at once. He uses the Oblivion and Oath-keeper Keyblades to devastating effect!

"I'M GLAD . . . I GOT TO MEET YOU.
OH . . . AND OF COURSE, AXEL, TOO. YOU'RE
BOTH MY BEST FRIENDS."

XION

Xion is something of an enigma, a former member of Organization XIII despite not being a Nobody. A Keyblade wielder created by using Sora's memories, Xion is in fact a replica puppet who was created to absorb Sora's powers. She resembles Kairi due to Sora's strong memories and feelings for her, though Xion's appearance changes depending on who is looking at her. After becoming friends with Axel and Roxas, she begins to form her own sense of self. She returns as a result of Xehanort's schemes as one of the Thirteen Seekers of Darknesses, ultimately betraying the new Oganization by deciding to help Sora and his friends.

Due to her unique nature as a replica, Xion's appearance changes based on who is looking at her. Sometimes she even appears as a puppet!

"GOT IT MEMORIZED?"

AXEL

Axel is a Keyblade wielder with a fiery personality. Formally a member of Organization XIII, Axel developed close bonds with Xion and Roxas, leading him to question his ties to the Organization after each of them left. Since then, Axel helped Sora and his friends on numerous occasions and even joined them against Xehanort and his followers. Though Axel is no longer a Nobody, he doesn't always go by his actual name, Lea. Unfortunately, this causes quite a bit of confusion! At the end of the day he's still the same person, a fierce friend and fiery ally, no matter what name he goes by.

Before becoming a Keybalde wielder, Axel used to fight with two chakrams and would use them to cast scorching hot fire magic!

"WILL YOU TAKE THE ROAD TO LIGHT OR THE ROAD TO DARKNESS?"

ANSEM THE WISE

Ansem the Wise is a well-known and respected researcher who was working to uncover the secrets of the heart. He built a facility and sought out bright young minds to recruit as apprentices in order to help him with his work. Unfortunately, Xehanort was able to become one of his apprentices and begin his own dark research. To atone for what he did to Riku, Roxas, and Naminé in his quest for revenge, Ansem works tirelessly to counteract Xehanort and his schemes, often helping Sora and his friends in the process. He is eventually able to work with some of his old apprentices that left the Organization in order give Naminé a body of her own.

With his name stolen by Xehanort's Heartless, Ansem the Wise hid his identity for a time and took on the name DiZ.

"SURPRISED? I GUESS YOU SHOULD BE. AFTER ALL, I LOOK JUST LIKE YOU."

RIKU REPLICA

A replica of Riku created by Organization XIII, this version of Riku clashes with both Sora and the real Riku in **Castle Oblivion**. Riku eventually reunited with Riku Replica in the Realm of Darkness and despite having been his adversary, Riku Replica agrees to join and help Riku.

Riku Replica has many of the same powers and abilities as the real Riku and can even wield some of Riku's weapons.

"QUIT TREATING ME LIKE A KID."

VENTUS

A young Keyblade wielder, Ventus lost a portion of his heart due to one of Xenahort's attempts to create the $\mathcal{X}$-**blade**. The experiment failed and Xehanort took Ventus to the Land of Departure, where he learned to use the power of the Keyblade. While there he befriended Terra and Aqua, two other Keyblade wielders who live there and studied the Keyblade under Master Eraqus. Eventually Ventus battled Vanitas, a being created by Xehanort from a portion of Ventus's heart. Their battle left Ventus greatly weakened and his heart eventually found its way to the Destiny Islands, where a young Sora accepted the heart into his own body to keep it safe. Later, Sora is able to awaken Ventus from his slumber, allowing him to fight as one of the **guardians of light**.

Ventus and Roxas look very similar! This is because Ventus's heart was still within Sora when Roxas was created.

"THERE'S DARKNESS WITHIN ME . . . SO WHAT DOES THAT MATTER? I KNOW I'M STRONG ENOUGH TO HOLD IT BACK."

TERRA

Terra is a Keyblade wielder who trained under Master Eraqus in the Land of Departure. While he is very strong, he is unable to control the darkness within him. This eventually led to him falling victim to Xehanort's plans, who is able to exploit the darkness within Terra and take over his body. While Terra is able to resist Xehanort's control somewhat, it wasn't until Sora confronted him that he was able to fight off Xehanort's control.

Even though Terra lost his body, his desire to protect his friends was so strong that it was able to animate his armor, creating a creature called the Lingering Will.

"MY NAME IS MASTER AQUA. NOW RETURN MY FRIEND'S HEARTS OR PAY THE PRICE!"

AQUA

Aqua is a Keyblade Master who studied under Master Eraqus. She has an incredible affinity for magic and can wipe out huge swaths of enemies with her powerful elemental spells. She was able to stop Master Xehanort from fully carrying out his original scheme to forge the χ-blade, though she became trapped in the Realm of Darkness in the process. There she wandered for years, fighting off the nearly endless amount of Heartless that dwelt within the realm. She was eventually rescued by Riku, King Mickey, and Sora and joined the battle against Xehanort as one of the seven guardians of light.

Aqua is actually the one who created Castle Oblivion by transforming The Land of Departure with the Keyblade called the Master's Defender.

"JUST BECAUSE YOU CAN'T REMEMBER SOMETHING DOESN'T MEAN IT'S GONE."

NAMINÉ

Kairi's Nobody, Naminé has a special connection to Sora and is even able to alter his memories. Because of this she was captured by the old Organization XIII and was forced to change Sora's memories of his friends. However, Sora was able to befriend her and together they managed to foil the Organization's plans in Castle Oblivion. Naminé is quite similar to Kairi, sharing her determination and kindness. While they were reunited as one person for a time, Sora and his friends are working to find a way for Naminé to ultimately gain her own body.

Naminé enjoys drawing and is able to channel her unique powers through the images she creates.

"WE'LL BE HERE WAITING FOR YOU!"

HAYNER, PENCE, AND OLETTE

A group of kids that all live in Twilight Town, Hayner, Pence, and Olette all become close friends with Sora and Kairi. Despite the fact that they are all just normal kids without any real powers, they've been able to help Sora and his friends a number of times on their adventures. Thanks to Pence's computer skills, Sora is able to travel to the digital Twilight Town and find a way to The World That Never Was. The trio even helps save Ansem the Wise from the clutches of the Organization! It just goes to show that even without magic or a Keyblade, all it takes is some teamwork and a good plan to make a difference.

The Twilight Trio love taking photos and have taken a bunch along with their friends!

"IT'S YOUR FAVORITE GUMMI ENGINEERS HERE, READY FOR DUTY: CHIP . . ." ". . . AND DALE!"

CHIP & DALE

A pair of chipmunks that work on **Gummi Ships**, Chip & Dale have accompanied Sora on almost all of his adventures. Their expertise has helped him navigate to different worlds and survive the powerful Heartless that inhabit the space in-between. But Chip & Dale aren't just Gummi Ship experts—their tech expertise allows them to create a variety of machines and gadgets that have helped Sora along on his journeys. Their inventions include a device that allows them to decode the data in Jiminy Cricket's journal and the Gummiphone, which allows Sora to stay in contact with his friends even if they're in a different world.

With Chip & Dale's help, Sora has been able to make tons of different kinds of Gummi Ship!

"OVER HERE! CRICKET'S THE NAME. JIMINY CRICKET, AT YOUR SERVICE."

JIMINY CRICKET

Jiminy Cricket has been traveling with Sora and documenting his adventures for years. The Roal Chronicler of Disney Castle, he was tasked by Queen Minnie with traveling along with Donald and Goofy while they searched for the wielder of the Keyblade. Ever since, Jiminy has tracked Sora's travels in his journal, though after they traveled to Castle Oblivion the journal was unfortunately wiped clean. Though he originally wrote the journal by hand, he now uses a new device called a Gummiphone.

Jiminy's journal is full of information about places, friends, and enemies that Sora has encountered on his adventures!

> "I AM NO LONGER A MASTER.
> I DOFFED THAT MANTLE."

YEN SID

A powerful sorcerer and King Mickey's master, Yen Sid is a frequent mentor and guide for the guardians of light. While he used to be a Keyblade Master, at some point he decided to put aside his Keyblade and focus instead on observing the balance between light and darkness. More recently he has acted as a teacher for Sora and Riku, administering them the tests required to become Keyblade Masters. Frequently stern and often admonishing, Yen Sid has nonetheless been a stalwart ally of the light and has worked tirelessly to prevent worlds from falling to darkness.

While Yen Sid seldom steps on the battlefield, when he performs magic it is a sight to behold!

"PRESTO!"

MERLIN

A wizard with a great deal of knowledge, Merlin has acted as a teacher for many of the guardians of light. In fact, Merlin taught Sora how to properly wield magic using the Keyblade. Merlin is also the keeper of the Hundred Acre Wood book, which acts as a portal to the world where Winnie the Pooh and his friends reside. But Sora isn't the only Keyblade wielder he teaches! Merlin created the Secret Forest so that Kairi and Axel can train to use their Keyblades in time for the final battle against Xehanort.

While he may not seem powerful, Merlin's magic is nothing to sneeze at!

"ACH! HOW DARE YE!? BACK OFF, YE FIEND! YE'LL NOT BE GETTIN' MY MONEY!"

SCROOGE MCDUCK

Scrooge McDuck is a successful business-duck that has traveled many worlds amassing his fortune. He spent years working with King Mickey creating a Gummi Ship highway system to connect various worlds, though their work had to be stopped when the Heartless began to appear. His other business endeavors include an amusement park and a restaurant. Despite what his name might make you think, Scrooge is actually a very kind and helpful person, especially when it comes to his great-nephews Huey, Dewey, and Louie.

Scrooge hires Little Chef to work in his Twilight Town bistro—which is a huge success!

"WOW, UNCA SCROOGE SURE WOULD BE PROUD OF US IF WE ACTUALLY WON!"

HUEY, DEWEY, AND LOUIE

Three young ducks determined to strike out on their own, Huey, Dewey, and Louie pop up from time to time throughout Sora's adventures. They can be frequently found running shops and selling anything from ice cream to Gummi Blocks. While they care for their Uncle Donald, the trio of brothers clearly look up to and take after their great Uncle Scrooge McDuck. Though they drive a hard bargain, the brothers have helped Sora keep supplied and ready to go on even some of his toughest adventures.

Before opening up their various shops, Huey, Dewey, and Louie started out making ice cream!

"YOU WON'T STOP A TRUE HERO!"

HERCULES

Make way for a real hero! Hercules is a demigod and fast friend of Sora, Donald, and Goofy. Together the three have butted heads multiple times with Hades, the Lord of the Underworld. Herc is always trying to prove himself worthy of his divine heritage and originally was hoping to become a god and join his parents Zeus and Hera on Mount Olympus. He eventually realized that he would rather stay with his friends and Meg, the woman he loves. Possessing massive strength and near invulnerability, Hercules is almost unbeatable in battle.

Even though he's a demigod, Hercules sometimes needs help getting around. That's where Pegasus comes in!

"I'M THE KING OF NIGHTMARES AND THE MASTER OF TERROR! IF YOU WANT CHILLS AND HORROR, YOU'VE COME TO THE RIGHT PLACE!"

JACK SKELLINGTON

Everyone hail the Pumpkin King! Jack Skellington is a master of fright—and a great friend to Sora, Donald, and Goofy. Sora has worked to save Jack's home of Halloween Town from not just Heartless and Nobodies, but the dastardly Oogie Boogie as well. Jack himself loves Halloween more than anything else—that is, until he learns about the magical world of Christmas Town! Jack has a big heart but is prone to getting carried away, which means it's up to his friends to get things back on track.

When Jack learns about Christmas, he finds himself with a new dream—helping "Sandy Claws" deliver presents!

"LIVE FOR TODAY . . . AND FIND MY OWN PATH . . . NOT MY FATHER'S . . ."

SIMBA

Simba is the king of the Pride Lands and a longtime companion of Sora. While Simba's world fell to darkness, Simba's heart endured in the form of a Summon Gem known as Earthshine, allowing him to assist Sora in battle. After Simba's world was restored, Sora, Donald, and Goofy helped him overthrow his evil uncle Scar and claim his rightful place as king. While Simba sometimes lacks confidence in himself, when it comes to protecting his friends he doesn't hesitate one bit!

Thanks to the Pride Heartbinder, Sora can summon Simba and unleash powerful fire magic!

"SO MANY PLACES I WANT TO SEE . . . I KNOW I'LL GET THERE SOMEDAY. I'LL FIND A WAY SOMEHOW. I'M SURE OF IT."

ARIEL

Ariel is a princess of the underwater kingdom of Atlantica and the daughter of King Triton. When the sea witch Ursula brings the Heartless to her kingdom, she teams up with Sora, Donald, and Goofy in order to prevent her world from falling into darkness. Ariel eventually falls in love with Prince Eric, a man she once saved from drowning. Though Ursula returns to cause more trouble, Sora is able to defeat her once more, allowing Ariel and Eric to live happily ever after.

The Ocean Heartbinder allows Ariel to help Sora in battle!

"JUST A LITTLE BIT OF PIXIE DUST. THERE. NOW YOU CAN FLY!"

PETER PAN

Peter Pan lives in Neverland, a magical world where no one grows old. Peter lives alongside a group of misfit friends called the Lost Boys and the fairy Tinker Bell. They often butt heads with pirate Captain Hook and his first mate Smee, which usually amounts to Peter and his gang pulling pranks and making a fool out of the two scallywags. Peter first learned of other worlds when Aqua, Ventus, and Terra visited Neverland. He would later fight alongside Sora to rescue Kairi from Captain Hook and help him seal Neverland's keyhole.

Don't forget Tinker Bell! It's thanks to her magic that Sora first learns how to fly.

"DON'T WORRY, SORA. YOU CAN COUNT ON ME. EVEN IF YOU FORGET POOH, I WON'T FORGET YOU."

WINNIE THE POOH

Winnie the Pooh lives in the Hundred Acre Wood, a special world that exists within an enchanted book. Pooh Bear spends his days with his many friends—Tigger, Rabbit, Piglet, and Eeyore to name a few—playing games and having fun. He's always on the lookout for honey, his absolute favorite food. Though his head is often in the clouds, he's always happy when Sora can stop by for a visit.

Pooh isn't the only one that likes it when Sora drops by!

"I HAVE TO TAKE MY FATHER'S PLACE TO PRESERVE THE FA FAMILY HONOR. I JUST HOPE I DON'T GET DISCOVERED."

FA MULAN

Mulan is a warrior from The Land of Dragons who fought alongside Sora, Donald, and Goofy to save her world both from the Heartless and from Shan Yu and the Hun army. In an attempt to bring honor to her family and protect her ill father, Mulan—along with Mushu, her family's guardian dragon—stole her father's armor and took on the name Ping so that she could join China's army. While she was eventually found out, she proved herself incredibly capable in battle and saved the Emperor from Shan Yu.

Mushu helped Sora, Donald, and Goofy on their very first adventure together!

"COMES WITH THE JOB. PHENOMENAL COSMIC POWERS! ITTY-BITTY LIVING SPACE."

GENIE

Genie is a magical spirit that used to be trapped in a lamp, forced to grant three wishes to whoever discovered it. Luckily he was found by Aladdin, who promised to free him with his third wish. However, when the nefarious Jafar stole the lamp and forced Genie to help him plunge the world of Agrabah into darkness, it was up to Sora, Donald, Goofy, and Aladdin to save him. Genie remained friends with Sora afterward, even fighting alongside him in battle whenever Sora summoned him. Sora would eventually return to Agrabah and help Genie and Aladdin defeat Jafar once again. Talk about persistent!

Thanks to Aladdin, Genie was eventually set free from the lamp!

> "SO MANY BOOKS, BUT NOT ONE ON HOW TO BANISH THE DARKNESS."

BELLE

Belle is one of the seven Princesses of Heart who were originally captured by Maleficent and her allies in an attempt to access **Kingdom Hearts**. She was rescued by Sora and Beast and quickly began researching a way to stop the darkness, though she was unable to do so. She eventually returned with Beast to his castle, where the two of them got swept up in Organization XIII's plans. She worked together with Sora, Donald, and Goofy to save Beast and banish the Organization from the castle once and for all.

Belle, along with the other princesses, is seen by Sora during his first Dive to the Heart.

"YOU! GET OUT OF MY CASTLE, NOW!"

BEAST

Though he was once a regular human, Beast was cursed by an enchantress due to his spoiled and selfish ways. The enchantress gave him a rose and told him that if he could not find someone to love him before all of the rose's petals fell he would remain a beast forever. Beast did eventually meet and fall in love with Belle, and when his world fell into darkness he set out in search of her. He was eventually able to return to his world along with Belle, though his strong will drew the eye of Organization XIII. He was able to fight off the Organization member Xaldin with the help of Sora, Donald, Goofy, and Belle, and together he and Belle were eventually able to break his curse.

Beast wasn't the only one transformed by the curse—the castle's servants were, too!

"BEST. DAY. EVER!"

RAPUNZEL

Rapunzel is from the Kingdom of Corona and is targeted by Marluxia from Organization XIII as she is one of the New Seven Hearts. Due to the special magic contained within her hair, she was kidnapped from her parents by Mother Gothel, who raised her as if she were her real mother. With the help of Sora, Donald, Goofy, and a thief by the name of Flynn Ryder, she was able to escape from the tower she was being kept in and eventually learned that she was actually the princess of the kingdom. She's no damsel in distress though—she uses her trusty frying pan to knock out enemies left and right!

For most of her life, Rapunzel's only friend was her chameleon Pascal!

"IT'S NOT THE SUM OF OUR PARTS, IT'S THE SUM OF OUR HEARTS."

HIRO

Hiro is a genius inventor from the city of San Fransokyo and a member of the crime-fighting squad Big Hero 6. When Heartless—and Dark Riku—invaded his world, he teamed up with Sora, Donald, and Goofy to fight them off. While Hiro may be young, his intellect and desire to help people make him a natural team leader, and thanks to his inventions, Big Hero 6 is able to keep San Fransokyo safe!

Check them out! The other members of Big Hero 6 are GoGo Tomago, Wasabi, Honey Lemon, Fred, and Baymax!

"PLEASE LEAVE. I NEED TO BE ALONE. I DON'T WANT TO HURT ANYONE."

ELSA

Elsa is one of the New Seven Hearts and the queen of the kingdom of Arendelle. When she was young she developed powerful ice magic but wasn't able to control it very well. This eventually lead to her running away from her kingdom, meeting Sora, Donald, and Goofy along the way. She was saved by her sister Anna from Hans, whose heart was filled with darkness. Thanks to her sister's love and selflessness, Elsa was able to learn how to control her powers.

Elsa isn't the only New Seven Heart in the world of Arendelle!

"NOPE! NEVER MET 'EM. DON'T KNOW ANYONE BLUE, GREEN, OR WHO'S ODDLY SPIKY."

OLAF

Olaf is a snowman who was brought to life by Elsa's magic. He met Sora, Donald, and Goofy while traveling with Anna, Kristoff, and Sven. The group then joined forces to look for Elsa. Olaf is incredibly cheerful and optimistic, though he doesn't know too much about the world, which can land him in a lot of trouble. If he's not careful he can fall apart and needs help to be put back together again, just make sure you find the right pieces!

Elsa also used her magic to bring another snowman named Marshmallow to life.

"TO INFINITY AND BEYOND!"

BUZZ

Buzz Lightyear is a toy from the world known as Toy Box. While he now accepts the fact that he is a toy, Buzz used to believe he was actually a space ranger. He is very protective of his friends and is wary of outsiders, acting suspicious of Sora, Donald, and Goofy when he first met them. He did eventually come to trust them after they proved themselves by fighting the Heartless and protecting the other toys. While Buzz's doubts almost cause him to fall to darkness, he is saved by Sora, Donald, Goofy, and Woody.

At first, some of the toys think Sora is from a video game called *Verum Rex*!

"YEAH, I AM A TOY. AND A FRIEND."

WOODY

Woody is a toy from the world of Toy Box. When Young Xehanort decided to research the nature of hearts, Woody's world was split into two and he was separated from Andy and most of his fellow toys. He worked alongside Sora, Donald, and Goofy to defeat the Heartless and Young Xehanort and find a way to go home. He is friendly, devoted to his friends, and believes that as long as they keep each other in their hearts they will never really be separated.

The other toys who get sent to the replicated world are Rex, Hamm, the Aliens, and the Green Army Men.

"DON'T BE SAD. WHEN YOU'RE SAD, IT MAKES ME SAD, TOO. AFTER ALL, WE'RE FRIENDS, RIGHT?"

CHIRITHY

The Chirithy are special Dream Eaters created by the Master of Masters to guide Keyblade wielders during the **Age of Fairy Tales**. Generally upbeat and friendly, Chirithy are closely tied to their wielder. In the event that a Keyblade wielder falls to darkness, their Chirithy will as well, transforming into a Nightmare. While most of the Chirthity were lost when their Keyblade wielders vanished after the first Keyblade War, Ven's Chirithy was somehow able to endure and eventually make its way back to him.

While Sora doesn't have a Chirithy, he has made friends with other Dream Eaters!

"THE FUTURE IS IN ALL YOUR HANDS. AS IS THE WORLD'S LIGHT."

MASTER AVA

Ava was a Keyblade Master from the Age of Fairytales and one of the five apprentices of the Master of Masters known as the Foretellers. She was given a Book of Prophecy by the Master and tasked with gathering strong Keyblade wielders and training them apart from the five unions. Ava instructed them that when the Keyblade War began they should leave to a new world in order to preserve the light. This group becomes known as the Dandelions and they successfully managed to escape the destruction of the Keyblade War and prevent the light from being fully consumed by darkness.

Before the coming of the Keyblade War, Ava was the leader of the Vulpes Union.

"IF THINGS DON'T CHANGE, THE ENTIRE WORLD IS DOOMED!"

MASTER GULA

Gula was a Keyblade Master from the Age of Fairytales and one of five of the Foretellers—the apprentices of the Master of Masters. While Gula was given a copy of the Book of Prophecies by the Master just like the rest of the Foretellers, he was also given an additional page that was not in any of the other copies of the book. The page spoke of a traitor that would work to bring about darkness, and it became Gula's task to find and stop the traitor. Unfortunately, Gula was unable to find or stop the traitor and the Keyblade War consumed the world in darkness.

Before the coming of the Keyblade War, Gula was the leader of the Leopardus Union.

"WE NEED TO DEFY THE MASTER'S TEACHINGS TO PROTECT THE WORLD!"

MASTER ACED

Aced was a Keyblade Master who lived during the Age of Fairytales as one of the Foretellers— the five apprentices of the Master of Masters that lead unions of Keyblade Wielders. Like the other Foretellers, he was given a copy of the Book of Prophecies that detailed the events of the future. He was tasked by the Master with assisting Ira as he led the other Foretellers, though Aced began to doubt Ira after the Master vanished. Aced would eventually try to defy the Master and tried to prevent the Keyblade War by collecting light, though he was ultimately unsuccessful.

Before the coming of the Keyblade War, Aced was the leader of the Ursus Union.

"KEYBLADE WIELDERS WILL SOON TURN AGAINST ONE ANOTHER. WHICH WILL LEAD TO . . . THE KEYBLADE WAR."

MASTER INVI

Invi was a Keyblade Master during the Age of Fairy Tales and one of the five Foretellers who presided over groups of Keyblade wielders known as unions. Invi was given a copy of the Book of Prophecies by the Master of Masters and tasked with watching over the other Foretellers and to act as mediator for their disputes. However, she began to act as a spy for Ira, sowing distrust in the other three Foretellers. Despite her best efforts, fights broke out among both the Foretellers and their unions, leading to the Keyblade War.

Before the coming of the Keyblade War, Invi was the leader of the Anguis Union.

"I WISH TO FULFILL THE ROLE BESTOWED UPON ME. THAT'S ALL."

MASTER IRA

Ira was a Keyblade Master and apprentice of the Master of Masters during the Age of Fairytales. He was given a copy of the Book of Prophecies by the Master of Masters, who told him that he should act as the leader of the Foretellers should the Master himself ever vanish. Ira is one of the few Foretellers who believes the Keyblade War foretold by the book of prophecies cannot be avoided. Instead, the Foretellers must work together to find a way to preserve the light so that it can survive once the war is over.

Before the coming of the Keyblade War. Ira was the leader of the Unicornis Union.

INTRODUCTION TO THE VILLAINS

Yikes! Now these are some pretty scary folks. You got your Heartless, you got your Nobodies, you've got some people bent on world domination! When it comes to the forces of darkness, you really have to think on your feet because these folks don't mess around. Well, okay, some of them do mess around but you know what I mean.

Anyway, make sure you watch out! Whether it's Xehanort and his schemes or Maleficent and HER schemes, these villains will stop at nothing to take over not just one world but all of them!

> "...THE HEARTLESS ARE DARKNESS MADE REAL AND DARKNESS LINGERS YET IN EVERY HEART." —YEN SID

THE HEARTLESS

The Heartless are creatures of darkness that want one thing above all else: hearts. Coming in many shapes, sizes, and levels of power, Heartless are a major threat to the Realm of Light. While most Heartless come into being when a heart is consumed by darkness, there are some that were created artificially during experiments performed by Xehanort and his allies. While the Heartless naturally seek out the hearts of almost any living creature, they have a great desire to find and consume the hearts of worlds. Thankfully, the Keyblade can seal away a world's heart, protecting it from the Heartless for good.

There are two kinds of Heartless: Pureblood and Emblem. All Emblem Heartless have a special symbol on them—something Pureblood Heartless lack!

"A SPIRIT THAT GOES ON EVEN AS ITS BODY FADES FROM EXISTENCE—FOR YOU SEE, NOBODIES DO NOT TRULY EXIST AT ALL." —YEN SID

THE NOBODIES

When a heart falls to darkness, a Heartless is created. However, those with strong wills also create a Nobody—a combination of the body and will left behind when the heart has been lost. Both less common and more dangerous, Nobodies are neither light nor dark. Instead, they are beings of nothingness, unable to truly feel emotion due to their lack of a heart. That said, given time and the right circumstance, a Nobody can gain a heart of its own, whether by experiencing true friendship or by having a heart forced upon them.

Only those with the strongest wills keep their original appearance after becoming a Nobody.

"DARKNESS IS A BEGINNING, YOU SEE, NOT AN END. AT BIRTH, EVERY ONE OF US EMERGES FROM DARKNESS INTO A WORLD OF LIGHT, DO WE NOT?"

MASTER XEHANORT

Cunning, ruthless, and nearly unmatched on the battlefield, Xehanort was a Keyblade Master without equal. His goal above all else is to access Kingdom Hearts and remake the world, and he will go to any length to achieve it. While Xehanort wields darkness freely, he is unique in that he sees equal value in both light and darkness. In fact, Xehanort has counted the light in the formulation of his plans, often using it for his own purposes without hesitation.

Xehanort wielded his weapon expertly, effortlessly weaving spells even as he attacks with his Keyblade. However, his powers extended well beyond normal magic and his Keyblade. Xehanort was able to expertly command darkness and often uses it to augment his own abilities. When using the χ-blade, his powers increase even further, allowing him to wield the powers and abilities of other versions of himself.

Powerful as he was, Xehanort's greatest strength was his mind. His schemes were so full of backup plans and contingencies it was almost impossible for Sora and his friends to thwart them. Each time a guardian of light managed to defeat him, Xehanort was always ready to try again, coming closer to success every time. It was only with the help of almost every Keyblade wielder that Sora had ever met—and then some!—that Xehanort was finally defeated.

After merging with the other versions of himself, Xehanort changes into a powerful and frightening new form!

> "IN THE END, EVERY HEART RETURNS TO THE DARKNESS WHENCE IT CAME. YOU SEE, DARKNESS IS THE HEART'S TRUE ESSENCE."

ANSEM, SEEKER OF DARKNESS

An incredibly powerful Heartless and one of Sora's first truly dangerous foes, Ansem, Seeker of Darkness was one of the many versions of Xehanort that exist. In fact, while he went by the name Ansem, he was actually Xehanort's Heartless, not the Heartless of Ansem the Wise. He attempted to open the door to Kingdom hearts by bringing together the Seven Princesses of Heart, though he was defeated by Sora, Donald, and Goofy.

At one point, Ansem was able to manipulate Riku into giving into the darkness within himself, briefly seizing control of his body. Though Riku was eventually able to free himself from Ansem's control, the Heartless would continue to haunt him for some time, a constant reminder of his own weakness. Their frequent

clashes created an odd bond of respect between the two, and Ansem eventually began to feel proud of how strong his former vessel had become.

As Xehanort's Heartless, Ansem factored into many of Xehanort's plans. Aside from Ansem's own attempt at opening the door to Kingdom Hearts, Xehanort tasked him with traveling to the past and contacting his younger self on Destiny Island. Afterward, Ansem remained on the island for years, lying in wait for the day that Riku and Sora would take their Mark of Mastery Exam. This allowed Xehanort to hijack the exams and almost lead to Sora becoming a vessel for Xeahnort's Heart—close call!

Ansem is often seen accompanied by The Guardian, a powerful heartless that aids him in battle!

"IF LIGHT AND DARKNESS ARE ETERNAL, THEN SURELY WE NOTHINGS MUST BE THE SAME . . . ETERNAL!"

XEMNAS

The leader of the original Organization XIII, Xemnas was the Nobody of Xehanort, created when he willingly gave his heart to darkness. In an attempt to grant hearts to the members of the Organization Xemnas, he tried to create his own version of Kingdom Hearts using hearts collected from defeated Heartless. However, this was merely

Xemnas is able to wield the power of nothing itself and can use it to create blade of pure energy!

a cover for his true goal—to use Kingdom Hearts to fill each of the members of the Organization with copies of Xehanort's heart, which would have allowed him to start a new Keyblade War. Thankfully, Sora and Riku were able to defeat Xemnas in The World That Never Was.

At first, Xemnas lacked a heart and was therefore almost entirely without emotion. This made him a calculating and dangerous enemy as he did not hesitate when making plans that would put his own allies in danger. However, as time went on Xemnas slowly began to gain a heart of his own, and with it he felt regret for taking his old comrades for granted. While he did ultimately work to further Xehanort's plans, in the end he felt one thing as he faded away: remorse.

"THIS WORLD IS JUST TOO SMALL."

YOUNG XEHANORT

A version of Xehanort from the distant past and one of the **Seekers of Darkness** that eventually clashed with Sora and the other Guardians of Light. This version of Xehanort was tasked with bringing the various versions of Xehanort that existed across time to the present so that they could act as the thirteen darknesses required to forge the χ-blade.

This Xehanort gained the ability to travel through time from Xehanort's Heartless, better known as Ansem, Seeker of Darkness. While this did allow him to travel forward through time, he eventually was sent back to his own time after being defeated in battle by Sora. It was this experience as a Seeker of Darkness that would subconsciously drive Xehanort to seek out the power of the Keyblade.

As a time traveler, this version of Xehanort possesses a very unique set of skills. He has much greater affinity for time magic, even resisting King Mickey's Stopza spell multiple times!

This younger version of Xehanort even has his own special Keyblade!

"I DID DECIDE WHO I AM. YOU SEE? WHAT I AM IS DARKNESS."

VANITAS

Vanitas was created when Xehanort ripped all of the darkness out of Ventus. Xehanort then made Vanitas his apprentice and taught him how to wield the Keyblade so that one day he and Ventus would fight, thereby creating the χ-blade. Vanitas is able to create Unversed, beings born from the negative emotions. Combined with his mastery of the Keyblade and command of Darkness, Vanitas is a truly formidable foe. He eventually became one of the Seekers of Darkness that fought alongside Master Xehanort.

Because Sora protected Ventus's heart within himself, Vanitas and Sora look A LOT alike!

"TRUE, WE DON'T HAVE HEARTS. BUT WE REMEMBER WHAT IT WAS LIKE. THAT'S WHAT MAKES US SPECIAL."

SAÏX

Saïx is the Nobody of Isa and a member of both the first and second Organization XIII. While he was originally a close friend of Axel before he became a Nobody, the two began to drift apart after joining the Organization. Feeling jealous of Axel's new friends Roxas and Xion, Saïx eventually became a Seeker of Darkness and fought against Sora and his friends. However, after his defeat, Saïx was recompleted and became Isa once more, allowing him to reconnect with his old friend Lea.

In battle, Saïx is able to channel the power of the moon to become nearly unstoppable.

"YOU TURN FROM THE TRUTH BECAUSE YOUR HEART IS WEAK— YOU WILL NEVER DEFEAT ME!"

MARLUXIA

A member of Organization XIII and eventually a Seeker of Darkness alongside Xehanort, Marluxia was the Nobody of Lauriam—a Keyblade wielder from the Age of Fairy Tales. While part of the Organization, Marluxia was tasked with rewriting Sora's memories in Castle Oblivion, though he secretly planned on leading a rebellion to overthrow Xemnas. As a Seeker of Darkness, he worked on tracking down the New Seven Lights as a fallback plan in case Sora and his friends somehow managed to avert the coming Keyblade War. He was eventually defeated once again by Sora and King Mickey.

In battle, Marluxia wields the deadly scythe Graceful Dhalia!

"I WAS REALLY JUST ALONG FOR THE RIDE."

LARXENE

Larxene was a member of both the original Organization XIII lead by Xemnas and the second lead by Xehanort. She was the Nobody of Elrena who was a Keyblade wielder during the Age of Fairy Tales. While she originally betrayed the Organization along with Marluxia, she was still chosen as a Seeker of Darkness by Xehanort due to the Keyblade legacy within her. Sarcastic and as quick witted as she was quick footed, Larxene often enjoyed poking fun at both her enemies and her fellow Organization members. She was eventually defeated by Sora in the Skein of Severance and underwent recompletion, becoming Elrena once more.

Zap! Larxene was an expert with lightning magic, firing out bolts as she zipped around the battlefield.

"THE FUN IS IN NOT KNOWING, ISN'T IT? WHAT IS THE POINT OF BETTING ON SOMETHING WHEN YOU ALREADY KNOW THE OUTCOME?"

LUXORD

A member of both the original Organization XIII and later the second Organization created by Xehanort, Luxord was a Nobody that had an obsession with games of chance. His abilities allowed him to manipulate reality and turn battles into card or dice games. Due to his odd fixation with betting and luck, he would often give his opponents odd advantages in order to make battles more interesting. He was eventually defeated by Sora, leading to his recompletion.

Luxord's weapon of choice was a deck of cards!

"THEN I SHALL MAKE YOU SEE . . . THAT YOUR HOPES ARE NOTHING. NOTHING BUT A MERE ILLUSION!"

ZEXION

Zexion was the Nobody of Ienzo and the sixth member of the original Organization XIII. Known as The Cloaked Schemer, Zexion was able to use his lexicon to both mimic the abilities of others and pull them into a different dimension. He was eventually defeated by Riku after battling him in Castle Oblivion, though he was recompleted and regained his original form. To atone for the things he had done as a Nobody, Ienzo then teamed up with Sora and his friends, helping them in their fight against Xehanort.

Before becoming a Nobody, Ienzo worked together with Ansem the Wise as one of his apprentices.

"I'M A SCIENTIST. EXPERIMENTS ARE WHAT I DO . . ."

VEXEN

The Chilly Academic Vexen was the Nobody of Even and a member of the original Organization XIII. He worked to create replicas, empty vessels that can be filled with the hearts of others. His work was crucial both to Xehanort's schemes and when it came to saving both Namine and Roxas after they had lost their bodies. While Vexen did join Xehanort's new Organization, it was actually just so that he could try to sabotage Xehanort's plans and make amends with his old master, Ansem the Wise. He was eventually recompleted and able to work alongside both Ienzo and Ansem the Wise once more.

Thanks to his massive shield Frozen Pride, Vexen was able to defend himself while also firing off powerful ice magic!

"DANCE WATER! DANCE!"

DEMYX

Despite being a bit of a laid back goofball, Demyx was the ninth member of the original Organization XII. Through a combination of music and magic, Demyx was able to control water with deadly efficiency, overwhelming his foes with waves of watery clones of himself. He was once again recruited into the Organization after it was recreated by Xehanort, though he was quickly benched. Vexen succeeded in convincing him to join the side of the light and together they were able to deliver the replica that allowed Roxas to be restored.

Demyx can use his sitar Arpeggio to create awesome magic—and awesome music, too!

"THEY THINK THE POWER OF LOVE WILL SAVE THEM? THAT'S THE STUFF OF POETRY, NOT PRACTICALITY."

XALDIN

A member of both the original Organization XIII and later the second Organization created by Xehanort, Xaldin was a Nobody that had an obsession with games of chance. His abilities allowed him to manipulate reality and turn battles into card or dice games. Due to his odd fixation with betting and luck, he would often give his opponents odd advantages in order to make battles more interesting. He was eventually defeated by Sora, leading to his recompletion.

Before becoming a Nobody, Xaldin was one of the apprentices of Ansem the Wise.

"MY POWER HAS NO LIMITS!"

LEXAEUS

Lexaeus was a member of the original Organization XIII and the Nobody of Aeleus. A man of few words, he has a keen mind for battle and tactics. He clashed with Riku in Castle Oblivion, and defeated him thanks to his immense strength and mastery of earth magic. However, Xehanort's Heartless within Riku took control and attacked Lexaeus, causing him to fade into darkness. Lexaeus eventually recompleted and became Aeleus once more, now remorseful that he worked with the Organization. He aided Sora in his struggle against the new Organization XIII.

While apprenticed to Ansem the Wise, Lexaeus's job was to guard the castle in Radiant Guardian alongside Dilan.

"THE HEART OF ALL KINGDOMS, THE HEART OF ALL THAT LIVES. A DOMINION FIT TO BE CALLED KINGDOM HEARTS MUST BE MY DOMINION!"

MALEFICENT

Maleficent is a powerful evil fairy from the world known as the Enchanted Dominion. She learned of the existence of other worlds after an encounter with Master Xehanort who also told her about the Princesses of Heart. She has desired the power of Kingdom Hearts ever since, seeking to use it to conquer each and every world. She has clashed with Keyblade wielders many times, though she has, on occasion, helped the forces of light if she felt it would advance her own goals in the long run. Recently, her attention has turned to tracking down a mysterious Black Box that once belonged to the Master of Masters.

When Maleficent embraces the darkness within her heart she can transform into a massive dragon!

"SEE? I TOLD YA YOU'D BE NEEDIN' OL' PETE!"

PETE

Pete is Maleficent's bumbling minion, working alongside her to conquer worlds with the power of darkness. Sora and his friends have had numerous run-ins with Pete, though his schemes are often harmless and foiled by his own mistakes as much as by anything else. Despite all that, Pete shouldn't be completely counted out, as his heart is strong enough that he can summon and command Heartless at will.

Pete wasn't always a villain! Back before he teamed up with Maleficent he used to be captain of a steamboat.

"NAME IS HADES, LORD OF THE DEAD, GOD OF THE UNDERWORLD, YADDA YADDA, HOW YA DOIN'?"

HADES

Hades is the Lord of the underworld and is obsessed with defeating Hercules and the gods on Mount Olympus. He's tried everything from recruiting Cloud to fight Herc to capturing Megara. Sora and his friends have managed to stop him at almost every turn, thanks of course to help from Hercules. That won't stop Hades, though. Whether it's helping Maleficent capture Princesses of Heart or unleashing the deadly Hydra, Hades won't rest until he's finally beaten that annoying wonder-boy Hercules!

In his most recent attempt to defeat the gods on Mount Olympus, Hades resurrected the titans, powerful creatures capable of giving the gods a real run for their money!

"WE JUST NEED A LITTLE MORE OF THAT OOGIE FLAIR!"

OOGIE BOOGIE

Oogie Boogie is from the world of Halloween Town and was one of the villains that helped Maleficent capture some of the Princesses of Heart. While he often talks about flooding the worlds with darkness, in reality he's mostly concerned with causing as much trouble as he can. He and Jack Skellington were frequently at odds, since Oogie would always go too far with his so-called "pranks." Jack, with the help of Sora, Donald, and Goofy, have been able to thwart Oogie's plans twice now, though who's to say the bag of bugs won't make trouble again one day?

Oogie's got friends of his own—watch out for Lock, Shock, and Barrel!

"MY FINAL WISH! I WANT YOU TO MAKE ME AN ALL-POWERFUL GENIE!"

JAFAR

Jafar was the royal vizier of Agrabah and one of the group of villains that worked together with Maleficent to capture Princesses of Heart. While he is briefly able to capture Jasmine, she is rescued by Sora, Donald, Goofy, and Aladdin. However, Jafar was able to steal Genie's lamp and used it to turn himself into a genie, only to be barely defeated by Sora and his friends, who trapped him in a lamp of his own. Due to the schemes of the original Organization XIII, Jafar is briefly able to escape from the lamp, though he is defeated once more by Sora and Aladdin.

While Jafar's magic is powerful, it goes off the charts once he becomes a genie!

"SO, WHICH WILL IT BE? THE KEYBLADE, OR THE PLANK?"

CAPTAIN HOOK

Captain Hook is a pirate from Neverland and a constant enemy of the mischievous Peter Pan. He first learned of the Keyblade when Aqua, Terra, and Ventus each visited Neverland and fought against him. He would later become part of the group of villains who team up to capture the Princesses of Heart in an attempt to obtain the power of Kingdom Hearts. Arrogant and quick to anger, Captain Hook rarely manages to get the better of Peter Pan, and was soundly defeated by Sora, Donald, and Goofy.

If there's one thing that Captain Hook is afraid of, it's the crocodile that ate his hand!

"THE SEA AND ALL ITS SPOILS BOW TO MY POWER!"

URSULA

Ursula is a sea witch from Atlantica who used to serve under King Triton. However, she was eventually banished and joined up with Maleficent and her group of villains. She was able to steal King Triton's trident and almost succeeded in claiming control of Atlantica before eventually being defeated by Sora, Donald, Goofy, and Ariel. She was eventually brought back by the power of darkness, though this time she used her magic to trick Ariel into giving up her voice. Sora and his friends were once again able to defeat her, banishing her once more. She would appear one last time to terrorize Sora and Riku during their Mark of Mastery exam, though she was quickly defeated—this time for good!

Ursula's pet eels Flotsam and Jetsam fight alongside her in battle!

"AND HERE'S MY LITTLE SECRET . . . I KILLED MUFASA!"

SCAR

Scar was a lion from the world known as the Pride Lands. He killed his brother Mufasa, the king of the Pride Lands and blamed it on his son, Simba. This allowed him to become king of the Pride Lands, where he ruled arrogantly and selfishly. He was confronted by Simba over his betrayal, and the darkness in his heart turned him into a Heartless. He was defeated by Sora, Donald, Goofy, and Simba, though for a time afterward he haunted Simba due to the doubts in Simba's heart. Once Simba began to believe in himself, he was able to defeat Scar's ghost, banishing him for good.

Scar didn't take over Pride Rock on his own. He had some help from a trio of hyenas: Shenzi, Banzai, and Ed.

"I HAD A ROLE TO PLAY. AND AFTER ALL THESE YEARS, IT'S DONE."

LUXU

Luxu was a Keyblade Master from the Age of Fairytales and the sixth apprentice of the Master of Masters. He was tasked by the Master with taking the Gazing Eye into the future, allowing the Master to create the Book of Prophecies. The name of this ominous Keyblade was simply "No Name." He was also asked to take and hide a mysterious Black Box, the contents of which are a mystery to all but the Master of Masters and Luxu himself. He was the only member of the foretellers that was not given a copy of the Book of Prophecies in order to prevent any temporal paradoxes from occurring. Shrouded in mystery, Luxu disappeared shortly before the Master of Masters and his whereabouts are unknown.

Luxu was given a Keyblade containing the Gazing Eye from the Master of Masters.

"'MAY YOUR HEART BE YOUR GUIDING KEY.'
I SAY IT ALL THE TIME; YOU ULTIMATELY NEED
TO DO WHAT YOUR HEART FEELS IS RIGHT."

THE MASTER OF MASTERS

The Master of Masters was a Keyblade Master from the Age of Fairytales. He took on six apprentices and was able to forge Keyblades for them from their hearts, and eventually putting them in charge of groups of other Keyblade wielders called Unions. His magic allowed him to send his Gazing Eye into the future on a Keyblade that he gave Luxu, which he used to view events that had yet to occur and write the Book of Prophecies. Eccentric and fond of making jokes, it's unknown to everyone—except for maybe Luxu—what the Master's true intentions are.

In the Book of Prophecies, written by the Master of Masters, it was foretold that "Darkness would prevail and the Light expire."

Hope you enjoyed this ultimate guide! There's always more to see—more friends to make and villains to save the world from—so be sure keep on the lookout for more books and adventures with Sora and his friends. The Kingdom Hearts Universe is vast and dense—this guide is just the beginning!